W9-BNA-561

READ ABOUT

Volcanoes

Jen Green

COPPER BEECH BOOKS

BROOKFIELD • CONNECTICUT

Contents

© Aladdin Books Ltd 2000

Designed and produced by
Aladdin Books Ltd
28 Percy Street
London W1P 0LD

First published in
the United States in 2000 by
Copper Beech Books,
an imprint of
The Millbrook Press
2 Old New Milford Road
Brookfield, Connecticut 06804

ISBN 0 7613 1173 4
Cataloging-in-Publication data is on file
at the Library of Congress.

Printed in Belgium

All rights reserved

Editor
Jim Pipe

Science Consultant
Dr. David Pyle

Series Literacy Consultant
Wendy Cobb

Design
Flick Killerby Book Design and Graphics

Picture Research
Brooks Krikler Research

What are Volcanoes?

Volcanoes are wonders of nature. They happen when red-hot rock from deep inside the earth comes to the surface.

When a volcano erupts (explodes), burning rock, ash, and steam shoot high in the air like giant fireworks.

Hot, melted rock called lava flows down the side of a volcano like a river of fire.

An erupting volcano is a very frightening sight. This volcano is throwing out red-hot lava.

Why is this house on fire? Answer on page 32.

Volcanoes are very dangerous. In 1996, a volcano erupted on the island of Montserrat in the Caribbean Sea.

Everyone who lived nearby had to leave. It was two years before it was safe to return.

Volcanoes do great harm, but they have good effects, too. They can make the soil good for growing crops. They also bring gold, diamonds, and useful rocks to the earth's surface.

A Volcanic Eruption

Volcanoes don't explode for no reason. Very strong forces deep inside the earth make them erupt.

The ground under your feet feels cold and solid. But the earth is not like this all the way through. Both dry land and the oceans sit on the earth's outer shell, the crust.

Deep inside the earth, the temperature is so hot that the rock flows like a very thick liquid.

crust

hot rock

very hot metals

Swirling currents in the earth push the rock up to the surface, where it melts.

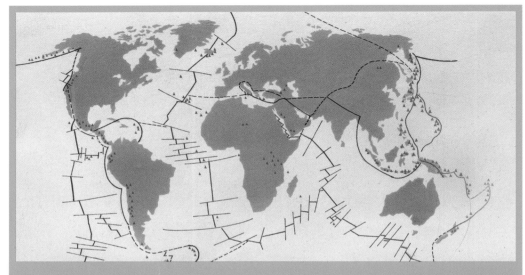

Most volcanoes happen where plates meet on the earth's surface. That's why some places have lots of volcanoes, and others have none.

The earth's crust floats on top of this hot rock. The crust is made up of pieces of rock, called plates. Many plates are thousands of miles wide. They fit together like a big jigsaw puzzle.

Where the plates meet there is often a weak point. The hot rock collects below this weak point in an underground space, the chamber. This fills up like a balloon filling with air.

The pressure builds. At last, the hot rock, or lava, bursts through. Clouds of ash pour out of the opening at the top of the volcano — the crater. Chunks of rock are hurled high in the air.

Red-hot lava pours out and spills down the side of the volcano. It cools and turns into solid rock. Layers of lava grow into a mountain.

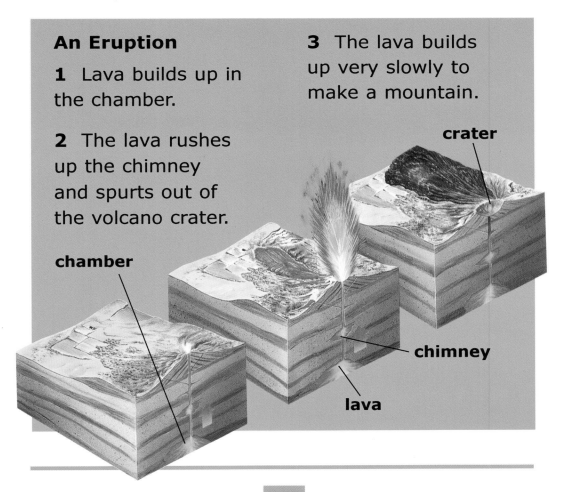

An Eruption

1 Lava builds up in the chamber.

2 The lava rushes up the chimney and spurts out of the volcano crater.

3 The lava builds up very slowly to make a mountain.

chamber

crater

chimney

lava

Volcanoes do a lot of damage when they erupt. Lava and ash bury nearby fields, towns, and villages. Buildings catch fire. The only safe place to be is far away.

In 1980, a volcano in Washington state called Mount St. Helens erupted suddenly.

Can you see that the top of Mount St. Helens has blown off in the eruption?

Before 1980, forests of tall fir trees grew on the snowy mountain before the eruption. Blue lakes sparkled in the valleys below.

As the volcano erupted, the top of the mountain blew off in a huge explosion. Rocks crashed down the mountainsides.

Afterward, the mountain looked as if a bomb had hit it. There was thick, gray ash everywhere. The trees were now stumps.

A cloud rose 20 miles into the air. It rained ash over most of the northern states.

The eruption damaged land and houses all around the volcano.

This volcano in Japan has erupted in the middle of a storm.

Types of Volcano

Violent • Gentle • Active • Dormant • Extinct

Not all volcanoes are the same. Volcanoes produce different kinds of lava. So they erupt in different ways.

Some volcanoes produce thick, sticky lava that clogs up the chimney from the crater. The lava traps a mix of steam and ash inside.

This volcano looks scary. But the most violent volcanoes throw out rocks and ash.

In the end, the volcano explodes. It hurls out crushed rock and ash. It's like a thousand trucks full of rock leaving the volcano every second — and traveling at over 300 miles per hour.

A river of lava

Other volcanoes produce runny lava, so they erupt more gently. The runny lava flows out quietly.

Volcanoes that have erupted not long ago are called active volcanoes. Some erupt all the time and never die down.

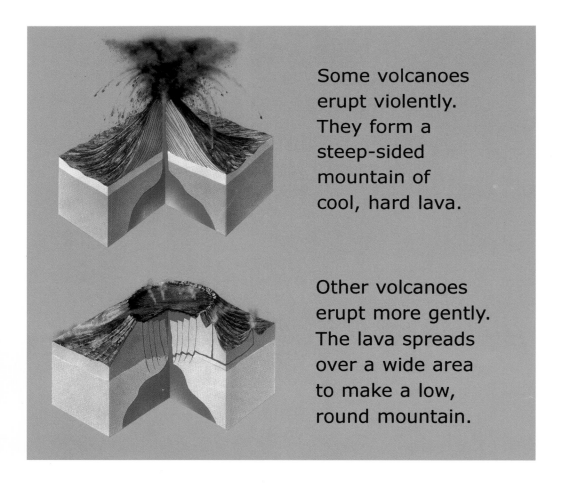

Some volcanoes erupt violently. They form a steep-sided mountain of cool, hard lava.

Other volcanoes erupt more gently. The lava spreads over a wide area to make a low, round mountain.

The volcano on the right is on an island near Italy. It has been erupting quietly for the last 2,500 years!

Some volcanoes stopped erupting thousands or even millions of years ago. They are called extinct, which means dead.

Other volcanoes have not erupted for hundreds of years. But steam rising from the crater shows they may erupt again one day. They are called dormant, or "sleeping" volcanoes.

A dormant volcano

An extinct volcano

An active volcano

Mount Vesuvius

The most famous eruption in history happened nearly 2,000 years ago in Italy. In 79 AD, a mountain called Vesuvius suddenly erupted.

Vesuvius had been quiet for a very long time, so everyone thought it was extinct. The town of Pompeii had grown up below the mountain.

A dog buried in the ash

When Vesuvius erupted a big cloud of hot ash rained down on the town. It buried people and animals in the street.

For centuries, the town was buried under thick ash. Then, in the 1800s, it was discovered again.

Experts found prints of bodies in the ash, which had become hard.

They also discovered houses with beautiful wall paintings and the remains of meals that were left when the volcano struck.

Volcano Damage

Glowing Clouds • Mud Flows • Giant Waves

Volcanoes do terrible damage around the world. They flatten forests and wipe out fields, towns, and villages — anything in their way.

Some volcanoes blast out thick clouds of burning ash and steam called glowing clouds.

These clouds are so heavy they drop down to earth and race downhill. They move much faster than flowing lava.

Cars aren't fast enough to escape some volcanoes. Can you guess what this truck is buried in? Answer on page 32.

Lava burns everything in its way.

A hundred years ago, glowing clouds fell on the island of Martinique in the Caribbean Sea. Everyone died in the town of St. Pierre except one man. He was in jail. It had no windows so the poison clouds didn't reach him.

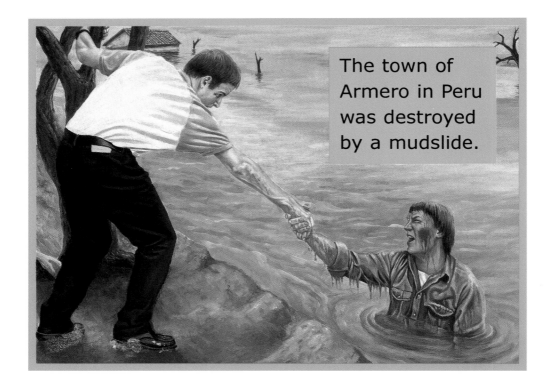

The town of Armero in Peru was destroyed by a mudslide.

When a high, snowy volcano erupts, the burning ash and lava melt the snow. The ash and water mix to make a tide of mud that roars down the mountain.

This tide of mud covers everything in its path. A town called Armero in South America was wiped out by mud in 1985.

Volcanoes don't only erupt on land. Many eruptions happen on the seabed, far out in the ocean. Volcanoes under the water can be just as dangerous as volcanoes on land.

An undersea eruption makes giant waves which race over the ocean. When the wall of water meets the land, it crashes over the seashore. Few people survive such a wave.

An underwater volcano erupts on the surface.

Some undersea volcanoes pour out so much lava that they become tall mountains. Some become so tall that they stick out of the sea to make new islands.

One cold morning in 1963, fishermen sailing off the coast of Iceland in the Atlantic Ocean spotted an amazing sight. A great cloud of smoke and ash was rising from the sea! The next day, a new island rose out of the ocean.

A volcano created the island of Surtsey in a few days.

Helpful Volcanoes

Farming • Rocks and Gems • Hot Springs

Volcanoes are very dangerous, but they are useful, too. Volcanic ash makes the soil good for growing plants. The ash contains all the minerals and nutrients plants need.

Over a long time, wind and rain break lava down to make new earth for growing crops. Then farmers plant the land around the volcano.

The minerals in lava help crops to grow.

Just after an eruption, the ground is bare and lifeless. But soon the wind brings seeds, and plants begin to grow. Birds and animals return to make their homes near the volcano.

When volcanoes erupt they bring rock from deep inside the earth to the surface. Some of this rock is very useful.

Oranges and lemons grow well in the good soil near this dormant volcano.

The amazing shapes of the Giant's Causeway in Northern Ireland were made by a volcanic eruption.

Granite is a hard rock that is good for building. Pumice is a white rock full of gas bubbles. People use it to clean their skin. It's so light it floats in the bath!

Granite

Miners also dig for gold, copper, and silver in old volcanoes. In some places they find diamonds and other gems, too.

Pumice

Diamond is the hardest material in the world. It is so hard it is used to cut and drill other rocks.

Diamond

In some parts of the world, hot rocks heat water deep below the ground. The water bubbles up to the surface to make hot springs.

The spring water is warm enough to swim in, even in very cold places like Iceland. We also use it to heat homes and make electricity.

What is this man swimming in? See page 32.

Volcano Watching

In the past, we did not understand volcanoes as much as we do now. Some people thought that when a volcano erupted it was because the gods were angry.

In ancient Italy, people thought that volcanoes were caused by the god of fire. His name was Vulcan and he was a blacksmith. His workshop lay right under a volcano.

People thought Vulcan was at work whenever the volcano erupted.

Volcanoes are named after Vulcan, the god of fire in ancient Italy.

The people of Hawaii believed that the rivers of hot lava were Pele's flaming hair.

Hawaii is a group of volcanic islands in the Pacific Ocean. The people of Hawaii believed that eruptions were caused by their fire goddess, Pele.

If a volcano rumbled and the earth shook, people said that Pele and her family were dancing.

Today we know much more about volcanoes and why they erupt. Scientists study them by measuring lava and taking samples.

They wear special clothes and masks that protect them from the heat and deadly gas.

Getting close to volcanoes is very dangerous. But taking pieces of lava helps scientists to find out what's going on.

Today scientists can often tell when a volcano is about to erupt. They watch for warning signs.

If a volcano is ready to blow, steam, ash, or gas may appear in the crater. The ground may tremble, or the mountain may start to bulge as lava builds up inside.

Lava can be 15 times hotter than boiling water. That's very hot!

Scientists can also tell when an eruption is about to happen by listening to the volcanoes. If experts believe a volcano is about to explode, everyone has to leave right away.

Sometimes people try to control the flow of lava. Bulldozers dig a channel for the lava, or build huge walls of earth to stop the lava from flowing toward towns or villages.

This bulldozer is building a dam to stop lava from reaching nearby houses.

Dormant volcanoes can surprise everyone by suddenly erupting.

All over the world, millions of people live close to volcanoes. Scientists are often right when they tell us when volcanoes will erupt. But some still erupt with no warning.

No one knows exactly when and where the next volcano will strike. That's what makes volcanoes scary!

Find Out More

Can you tell if a volcano is active, dormant, or extinct?
Look at pictures **a**, **b**, **c**, and **d** and see if you can figure
out what volcanoes they show. The answers are on page 32.

UNUSUAL WORDS

Here we explain some words you
may have read in this book.

Active A volcano that is
erupting.

Chamber A large space under
a volcano in which lava
collects.

Chimney The pipe
inside a volcano
leading up from the
chamber. Lava flows
through the chimney in
an eruption.

Crater The opening in the top of
a volcano where lava, ash, and
steam escape.

Crust The outer layer of the earth.

Erupt To explode.

Dormant A volcano that has not
erupted recently, but may erupt
again. Dormant means sleeping.

Extinct A volcano that has not
erupted for thousands or millions
of years. Extinct means dead.

Glowing cloud A thick cloud of
burning ash and gas given
off by some volcanoes.

Lava Hot, melted rock
that erupts from a
volcano.

Spring A place where
underground water comes to
the surface.

Volcano An opening in the
earth's crust through which hot
rock from deep inside the earth
escapes to the surface. Many
volcanoes are tall mountains.

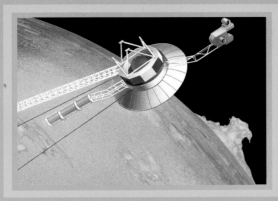

Volcanoes in Space
There are volcanoes on other planets, too. The biggest is on Mars and it's called Olympus Mons. It's bigger than New York state. But it hasn't erupted for millions of years.

STRANGE VOLCANO FACTS
Mount Etna, Italy
Volcanoes make different noises. Lava on Mount Etna (*right*) sounds like rocks being poured onto the ground. Other volcanoes make gurgling or rushing noises.

Krakatau, Indonesia
When this volcano erupted in 1883, it started a giant wave that traveled several times around the world.

Mount Pinatubo, Philippines
This volcano erupted in 1991. But water still washes ash off the volcano when it rains. Nearby villages are built on stilts to avoid the heaps of ash.

Index

ANSWERS TO PICTURE QUESTIONS

Page 4 Red-hot lava flowed down the side of the volcano and set the house on fire.
Page 16 The truck is buried in lava. Lava flows like a liquid when it is hot. When it cools it becomes very hard.

Page 24 The man is swimming in a hot spring — and he's wiped mud on himself. The mud in some hot springs can be good for your skin.
Page 30 Volcano **a** is active, volcano **b** is dormant, volcano **c** is extinct, and volcano **d** is active.

Illustrators: James Field – SGA, Pete Roberts – Allied Artists, Mike Saunders and Aziz Khan.
Photocredits: *Abbreviations: t-top, m-middle, b-bottom, r-right, l-left, c-center.* Cover and Pages 4, 8-9, 11, 27, 28 & 31m – Frank Spooner Pictures; 8, 9 & 23 – Eye Ubiquitous; 10, 16, 17, 19, 21 & 29 – Rex Features; 1, 3 & 13 – Oxford Scientific Films; 22 & 31b – James Davis Travel Photography.